Easy Piano
BEST of GREEN DAY
16 GREATEST HITS
Arranged by Carol Matz

ALBUM ARTWORK:

American Idiot © 2004 Reprise Records for the U.S. and WEA International Inc. for the world outside the U.S.

Warning © 2000 Reprise Records for the U.S. and WEA International Inc. for the world outside the U.S.

Nimrod © 1997 Reprise Records for the U.S. and WEA International Inc. for the world outside the U.S.

International Superhits! © 2001 Reprise Records for the U.S. and WEA International Inc. for the world outside the U.S.

Dookie © 1994 Reprise Records for the U.S. and WEA International Inc. for the world outside the U.S.

Copyright © MMVI by Alfred Publishing Co., Inc.
All rights reserved. Printed in USA.

ISBN-10: 0-7390-4254-8
ISBN-13: 978-0-7390-4254-0

BOULEVARD OF BROKEN DREAMS

Arranged by Carol Matz

Words by Billie Joe
Music by Green Day

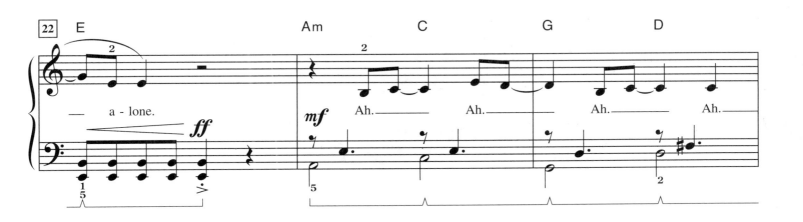

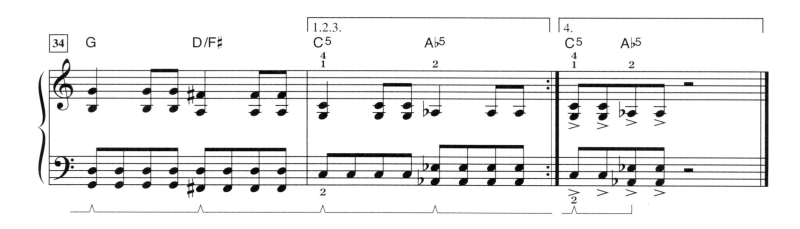

GOOD RIDDANCE
(Time of Your Life)

Arranged by Carol Matz

Lyrics by Billie Joe
Music by Billie Joe and Green Day

Verses 1 & 2:

1. An - oth - er turn - ing point,—— a fork stuck in—— the road.
2. So take the pho - to - graphs—— and still frames in—— your mind.

Time grabs you by the wrist,—— di - rects you where—— to go.
Hang it on a shelf—— in good health and—— good time.

So make the best of—— this Tat - toos of mem - o - ries, and

ped. simile

WAKE ME UP WHEN SEPTEMBER ENDS

Arranged by Carol Matz

Words by Billie Joe
Music by Green Day

9

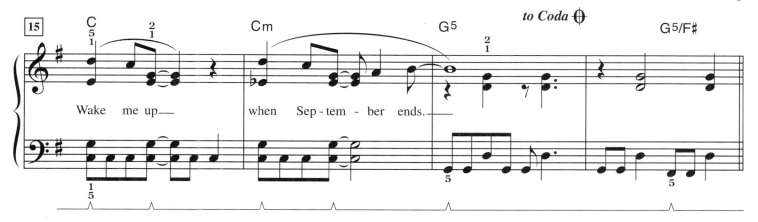

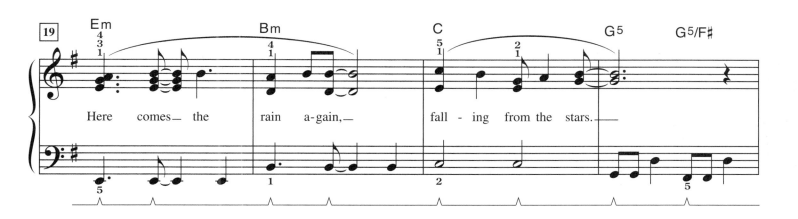

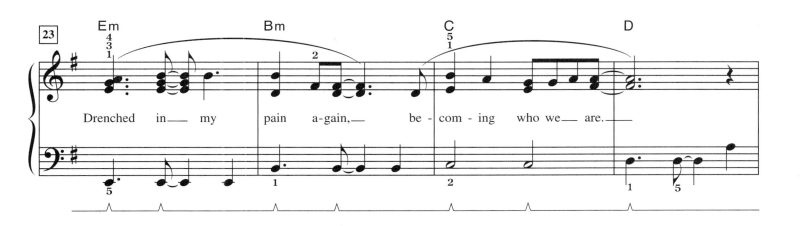

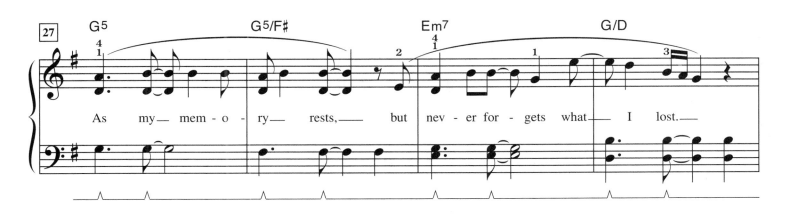

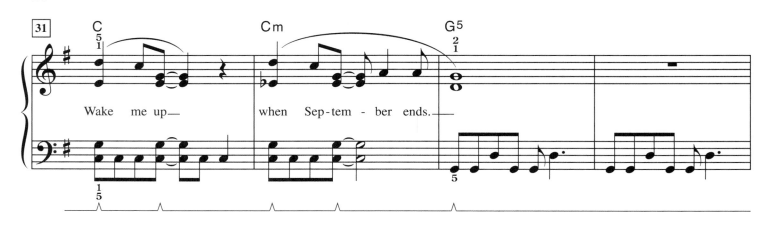

Wake me up— when Sep-tem - ber ends.—

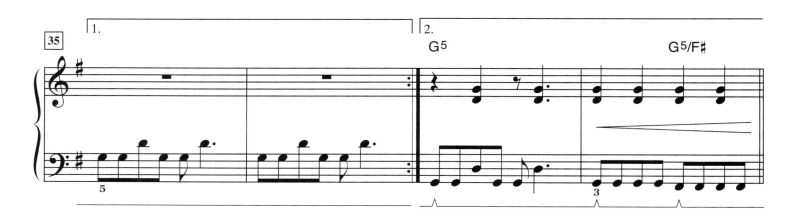

Instrumental:

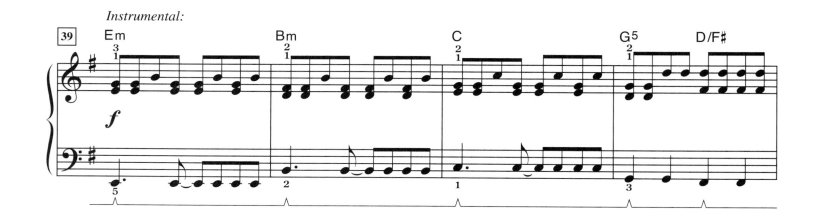

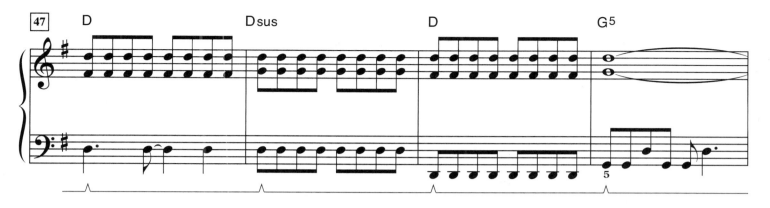

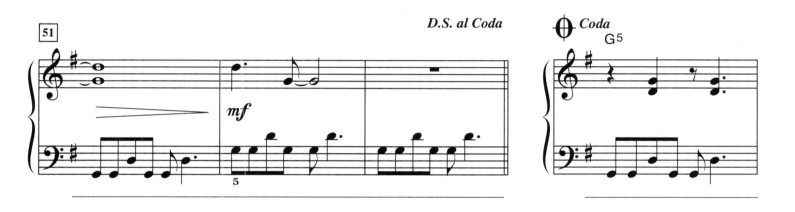

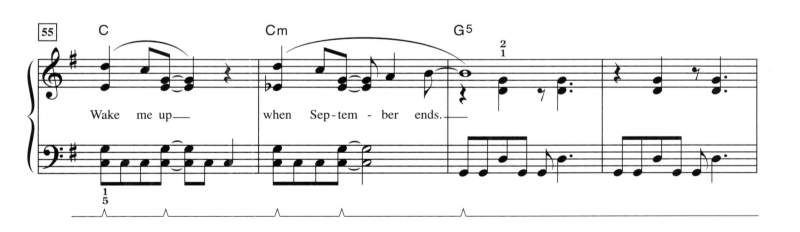

Wake me up—— when Sep-tem - ber ends.——

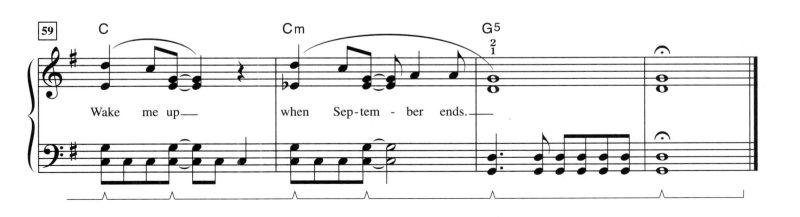

Wake me up—— when Sep-tem - ber ends.——

MISERY

Arranged by Carol Matz

Lyrics by Billie Joe
Music by Green Day

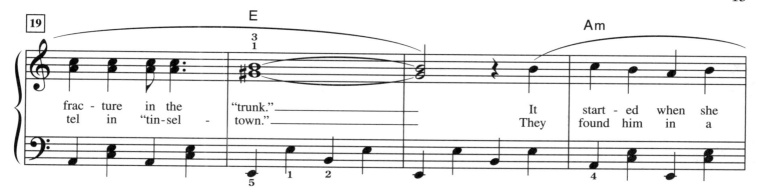

frac - ture in the "trunk."
tel in "tin-sel - town."

It start - ed when she
They found him in a

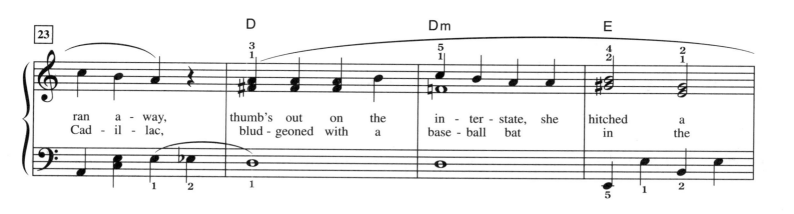

ran a - way,
Cad - il - lac,

thumb's out on the
blud - geoned with a

in - ter - state, she
base - ball bat

hitched a
in the

ride to mis-er - y.
name of mis-er - y.

"Mis - ter Whir-ly" had a
Gin - a hit the

cat - a - stroph-ic
road to New York

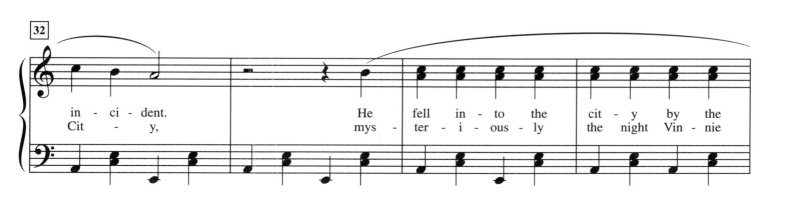

in - ci - dent.
Cit - y,

He fell in - to the
mys - ter - i - ous-ly

cit - y by the
the night Vin - nie

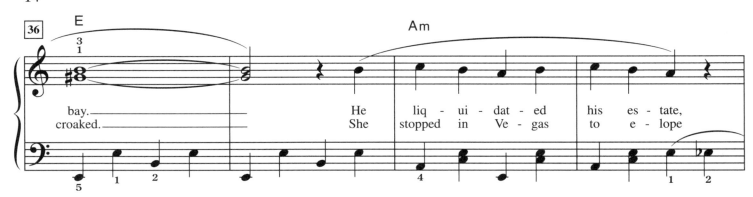

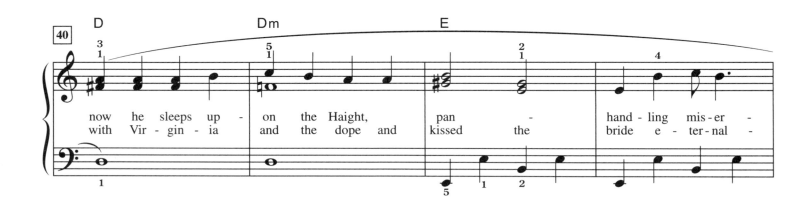

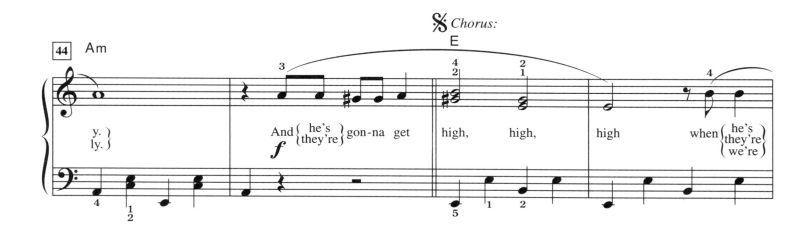

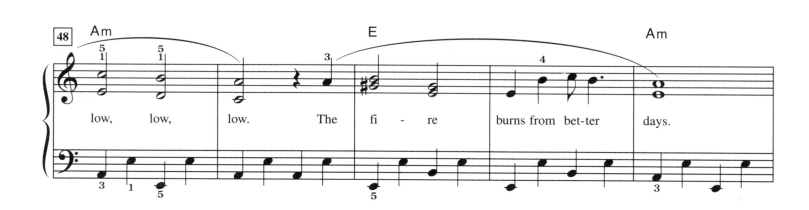

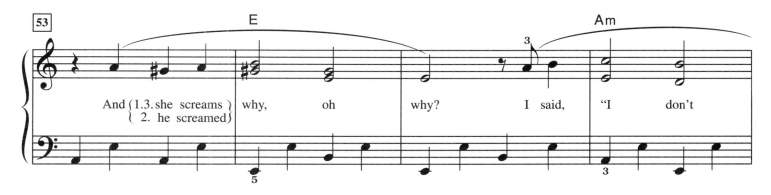

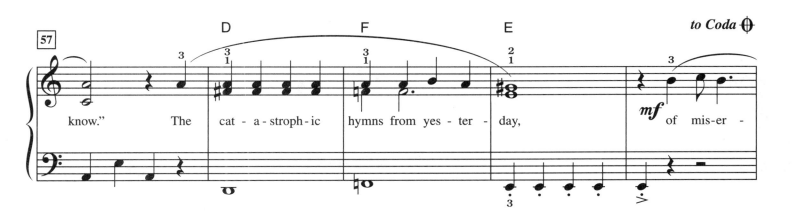

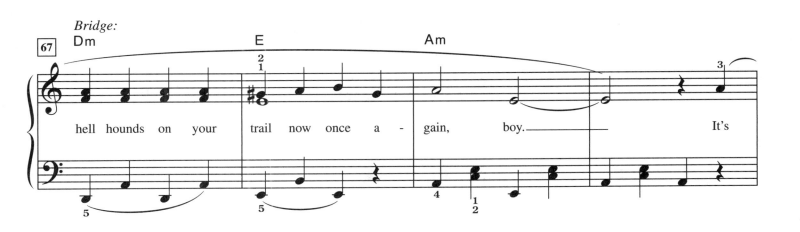

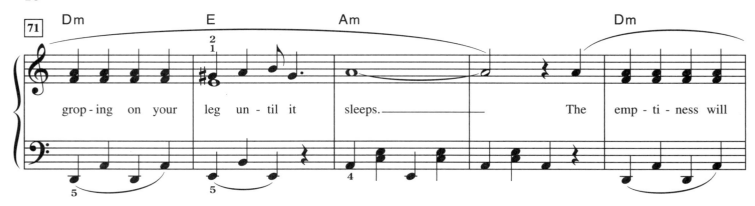

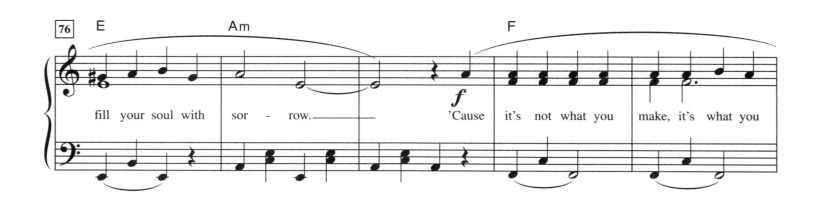

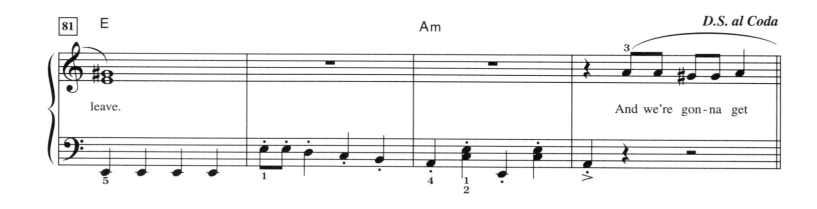

BASKET CASE

Arranged by Carol Matz

Lyrics by Billie Joe
Music by Green Day

LONGVIEW

Arranged by Carol Matz

Lyrics by Billie Joe
Music by Green Day

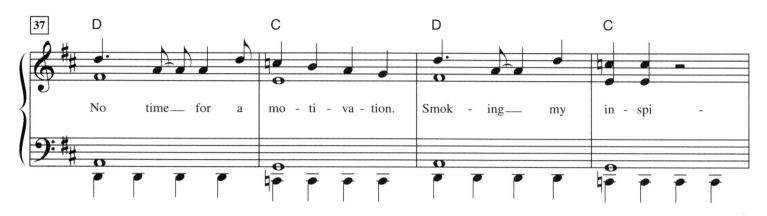

No time— for a mo - ti - va - tion. Smok - ing— my in - spi -

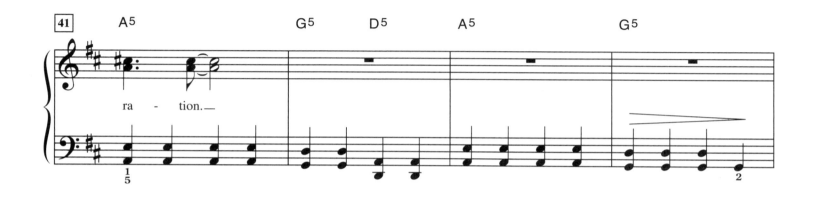

ra - tion.—

D.S. al Coda

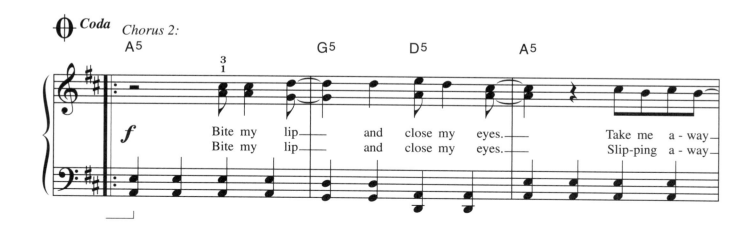

Coda   Chorus 2:

Bite my lip— and close my eyes.—   Take me a - way
Bite my lip— and close my eyes.—   Slip-ping a - way

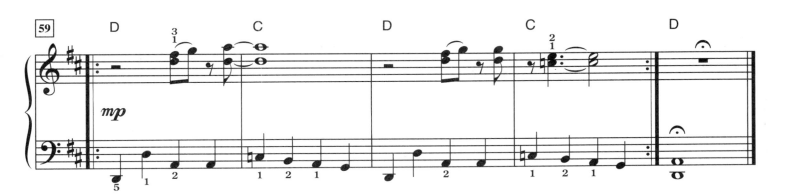

Verse 2:
Peel me off this velcro seat and get me moving.
I sure as hell can't do it by myself.
I'm feeling like a dog in heat
Barred indoors from the summer street.
I locked the door to my own cell
And I lost the key.

Verse 3:
I sit around and watch the phone but no one's calling.
Call me pathetic, call me what you will.
My mother says to get a job,
But she don't like the one she's got.
When masturbation's lost its fun
You're f***ing lonely.

WHEN I COME AROUND

Arranged by Carol Matz

Lyrics by Billie Joe
Music by Green Day

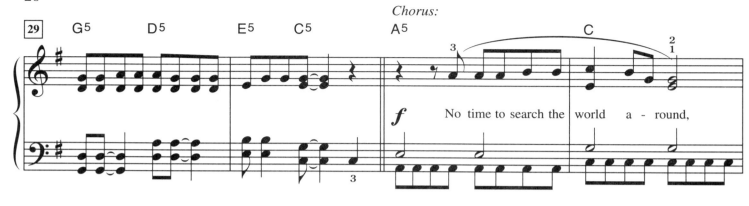

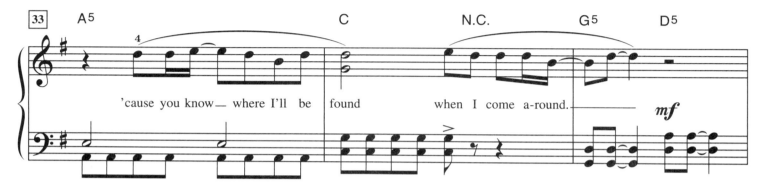

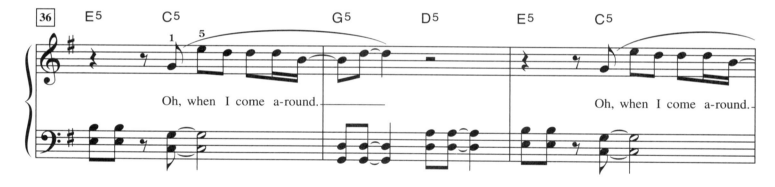

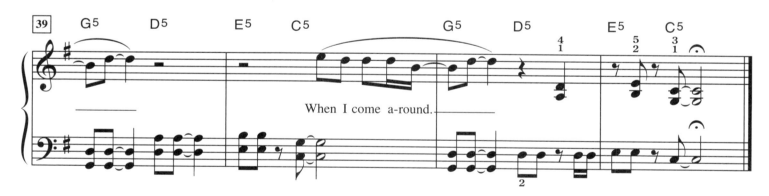

Verse 2:
I heard it all before,
So don't knock down my door.
I'm a loser and a user so
I don't need no accuser
To try and slag me down, because I
Know you're right.
So go do what you like.
Make sure you do it wise.
You may find out that your
Self-doubt means nothing was ever there.
You can't go forcing something
If it's just not right.

WAITING

Arranged by Carol Matz

Words and Music by Billie Joe,
Anthony Hatch and Green Day

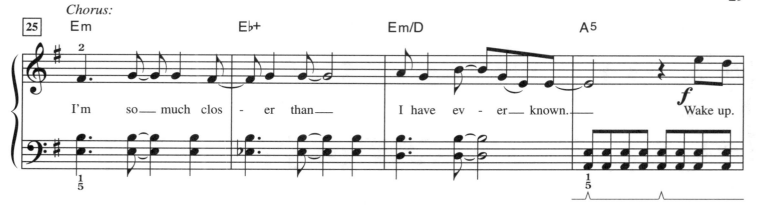

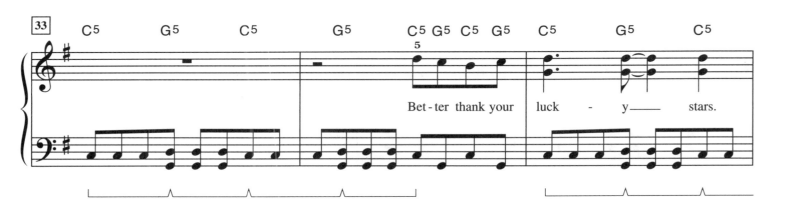

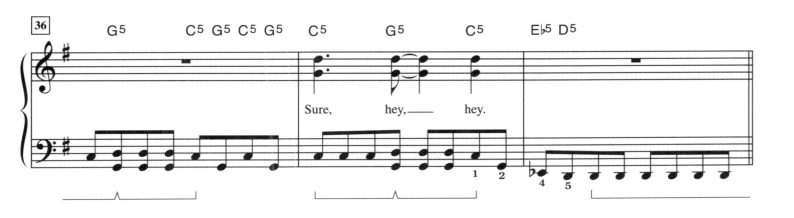

30

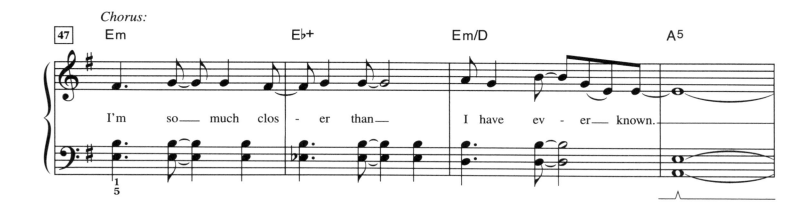

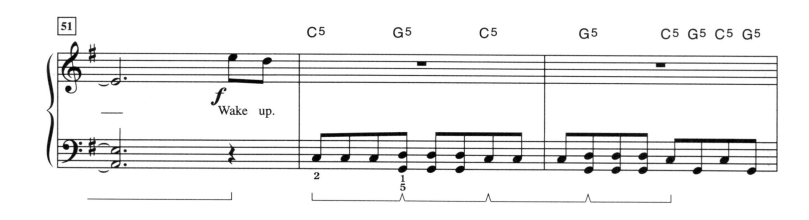

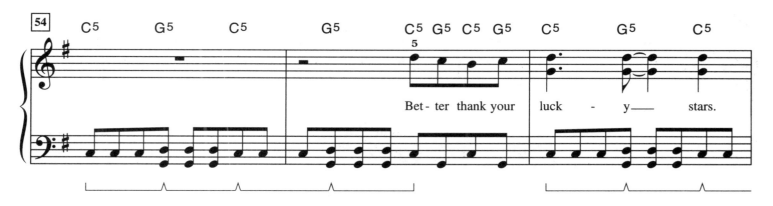

D.C. al Coda

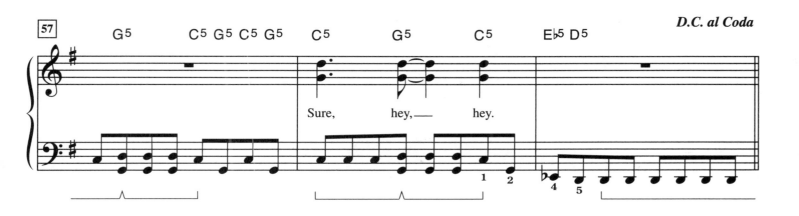

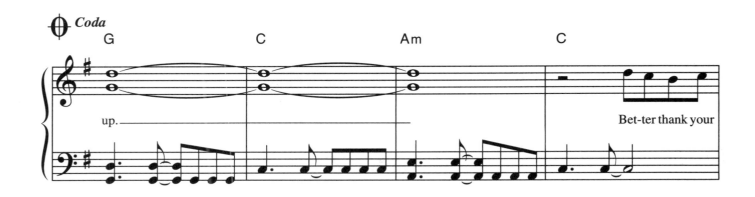

WARNING

Arranged by Carol Matz

Words by Billie Joe
Music by Green Day

Moderately

Verses 1, 2 & 3:

1. This is a pub - lic ser - vice an - nounce - ment.
2. 3. *see additional lyrics*

This is on - ly a test.

E - mer - gen - cy, e - vac - u - a - tion, pro - test.

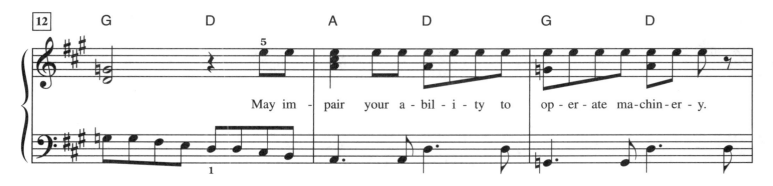

May im - pair your a - bil - i - ty to op - er - ate ma-chin-er - y.

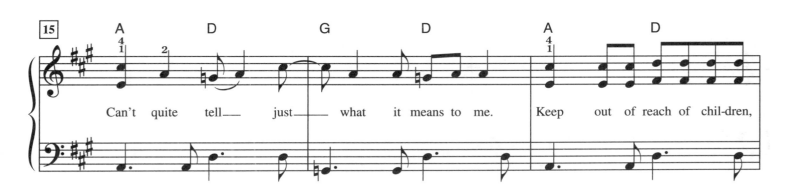

Can't quite tell___ just___ what it means to me. Keep out of reach of chil-dren,

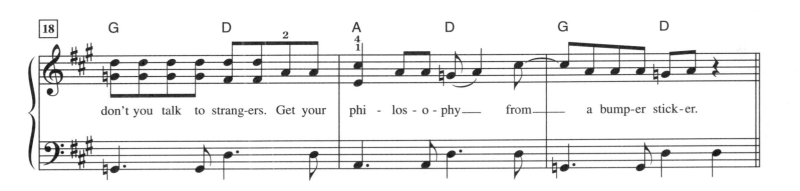

don't you talk to strang-ers. Get your phi - los - o - phy___ from___ a bump-er stick-er.

Chorus:

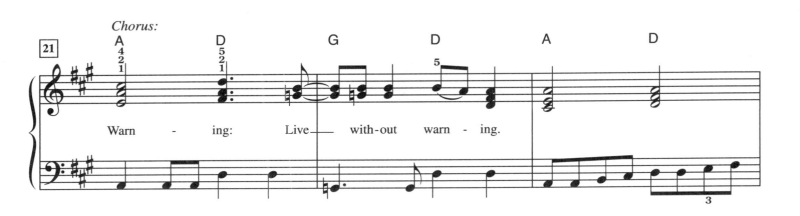

Warn ___ - ing: Live___ with-out warn ___ - ing.

34

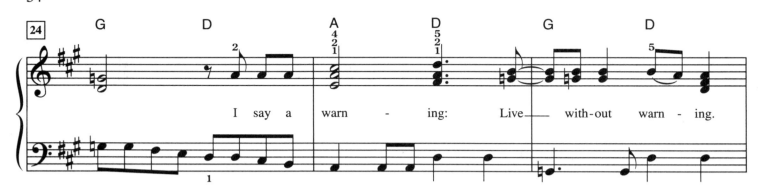

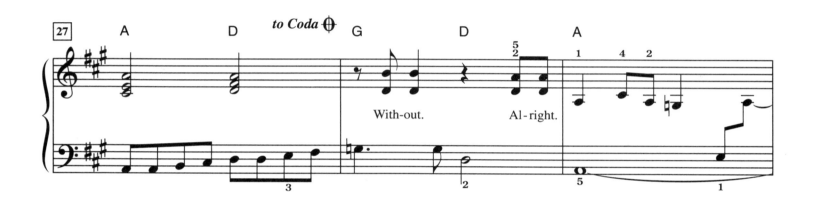

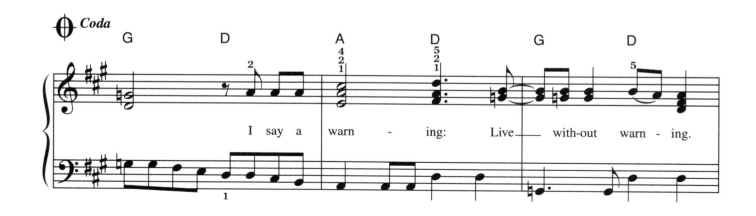

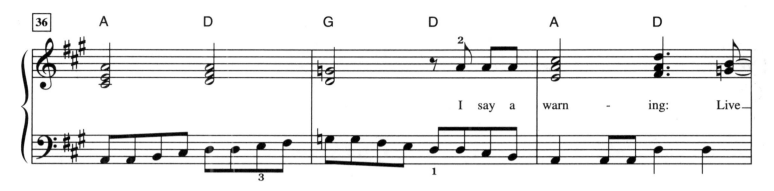

I say a warn - ing: Live

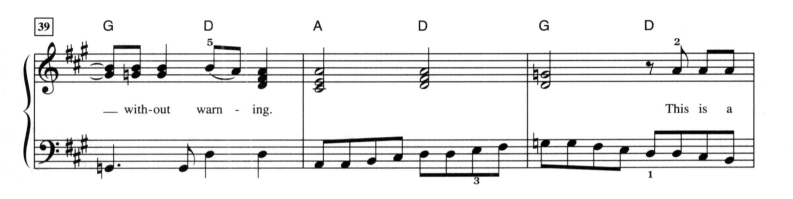

— with-out warn - ing. This is a

pub - lic ser - vice an-nounce-ment. This is on - ly a test.

Verses 2 & 3:
Better homes and safety-sealed communities?
Did you remember to pay the utility?
Caution: Police line. You better not cross.
Is it the cop or am I the one that's really dangerous?
Sanitation, expiration date, question everything?
Or shut up and be a victim of authority.

GEEK STINK BREATH

Arranged by Carol Matz

Lyrics by Billie Joe
Music by Green Day

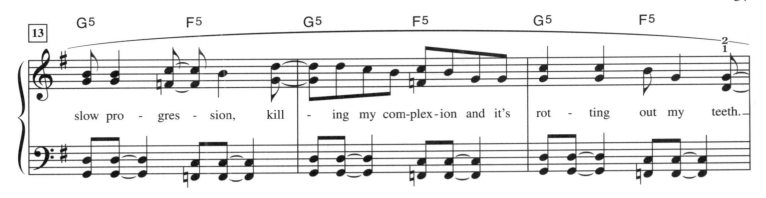

slow pro - gres - sion, kill - ing my com-plex-ion and it's rot - ting out my teeth.

Chorus:

I'm on a roll, — no self con-trol, — I'm

blow-ing off steam — with meth - am-phet - a-mine. — Well, don't know what I want — and that's

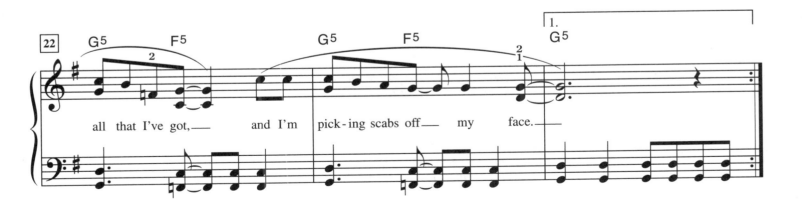

all that I've got, — and I'm pick-ing scabs off — my face. —

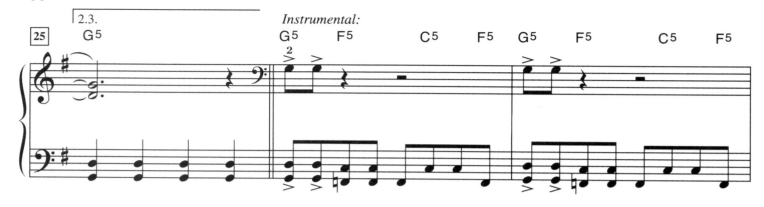

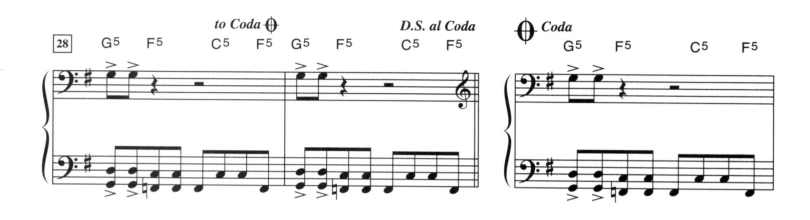

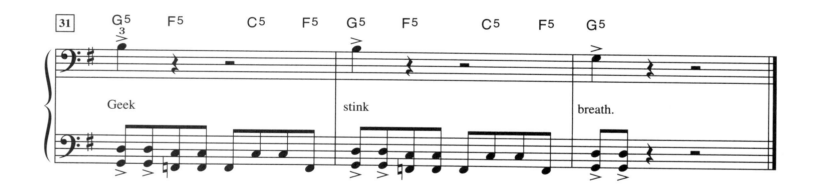

Verse 2:
Every hour my blood is turning sour
And my pulse is beating out of time.
I found a treasure filled with sick pleasure
And it sits on a thin, white line.

Verse 3:
I'm on a mission. I got no decision,
Like a cripple running the rat race.
Wish in one hand and s**t in the other,
And see which one gets filled first.

WALKING CONTRADICTION

Arranged by Carol Matz

Lyrics by Billie Joe
Music by Green Day

41

Verse 2:
Standards set and broken all the time,
Control the chaos behind a gun.
Call it as I see it, even if
I was born deaf, blind and dumb.
Losers winning big on the lottery,
Rehab rejects still sniffing glue.
Constant refutation with myself,
I'm a victim of a catch 22.

POPROCKS & COKE

Arranged by Carol Matz

Words by Billie Joe
Music by Green Day

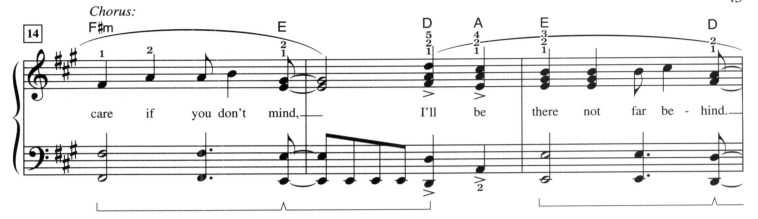

Chorus:

care if you don't mind,— I'll be there not far be - hind.

— I will dare keep in mind,— I'll be there for

you.———

mf

to Coda ⊕

D.C. al Coda

⊕ **Coda**

Verse 4:

If you— should fall,— you know— I'll

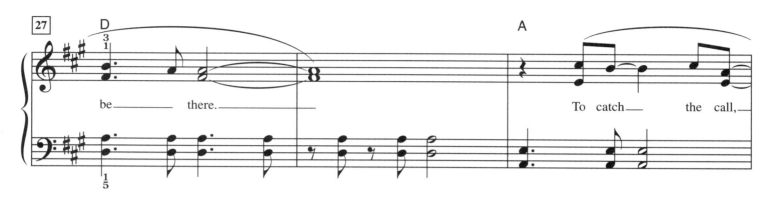

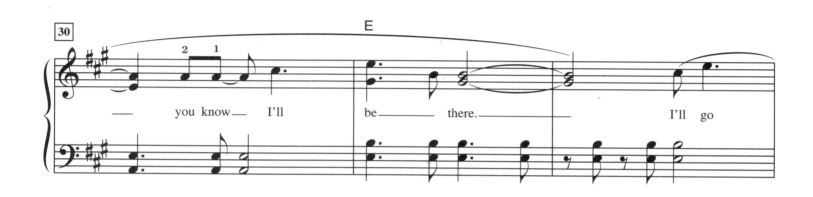

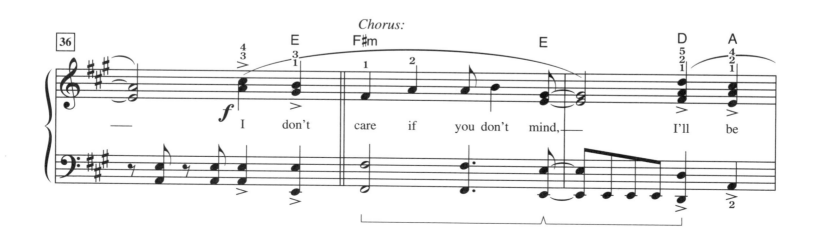

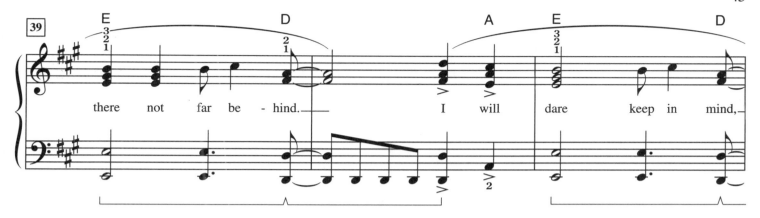

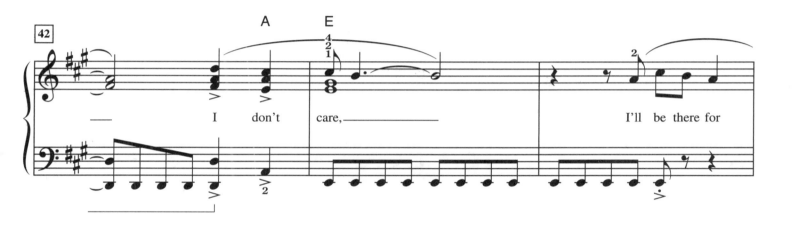

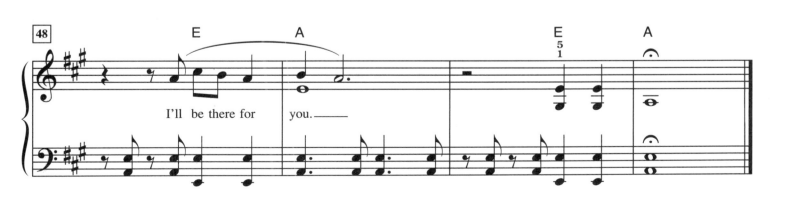

MACY'S DAY PARADE

Arranged by Carol Matz

Words by Billie Joe
Music by Green Day

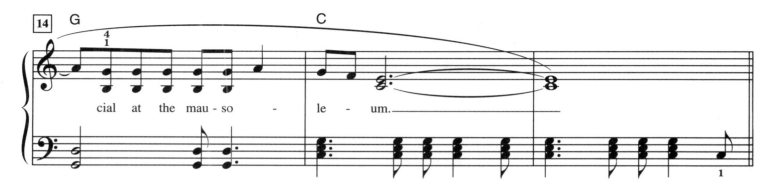

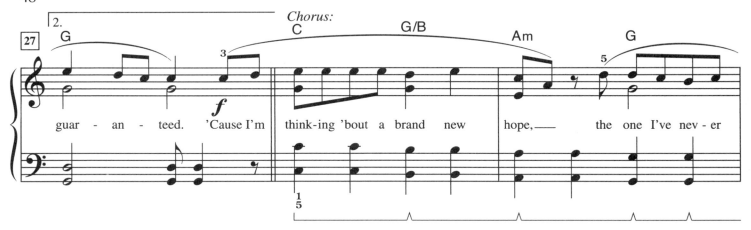

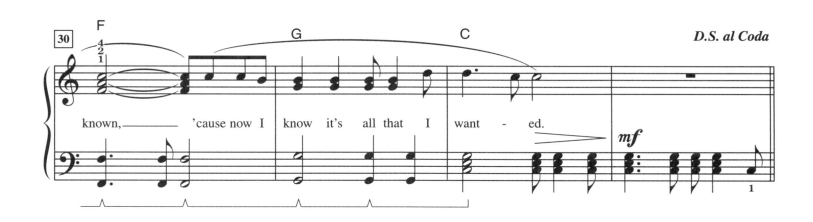

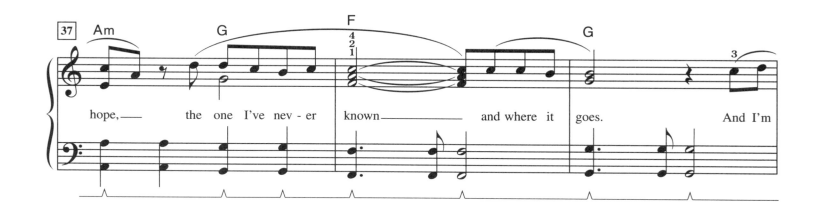

think-ing 'bout the on - ly road,___ the one I've nev - er known___ and where it

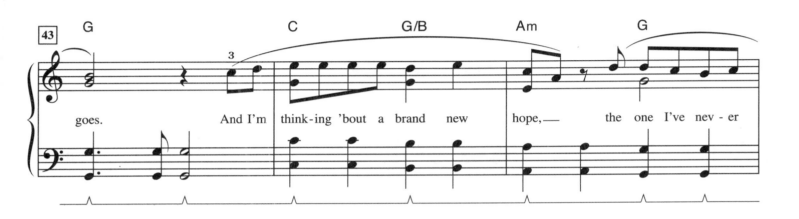

goes. And I'm think-ing 'bout a brand new hope,___ the one I've nev - er

known,___ 'cause now I know it's all that I want - ed.___

Verse 2:
When I was a kid I thought
I wanted all the things that I haven't got.
Oh, but I learned the hardest way.
Then I realized what it took
To tell the difference between thieves and crooks.
Let's learn, me and you.

HOLIDAY

Arranged by Carol Matz

Words by Billie Joe
Music by Green Day

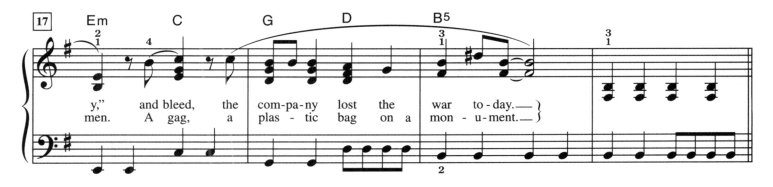

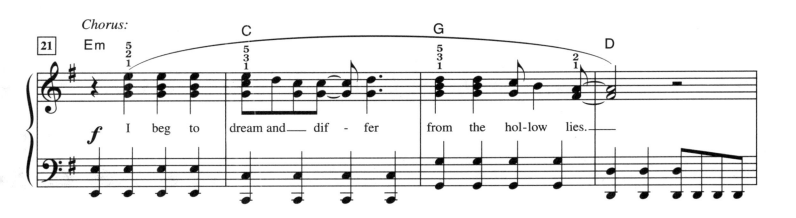

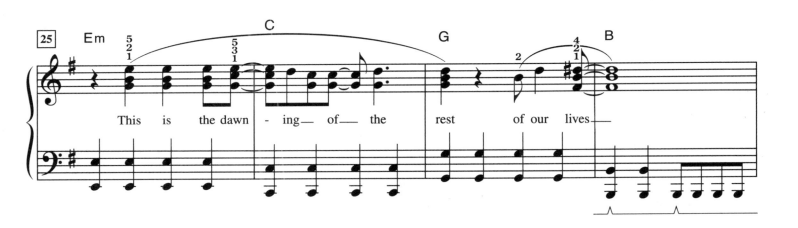

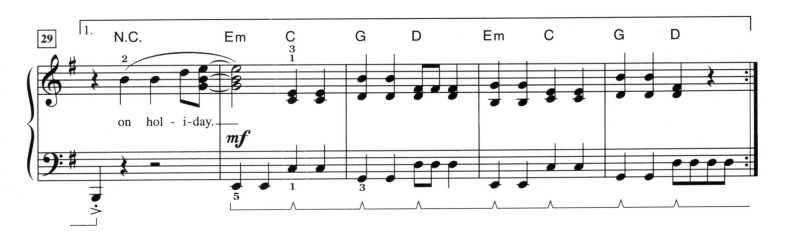

53

Bridge (spoken lyrics):
The representative from California has the floor.
Zieg Heil to the President gasman,
Bombs away is your punishment.
Pulverize the Eiffel Towers,
Who criticize your government.
Bang, bang goes the broken glass and
Kill all the f**s that don't agree.
Trials by fire setting fire
Is not a way that's meant for me.

AMERICAN IDIOT

Arranged by Carol Matz

Words by Billie Joe
Music by Green Day

Verses 1 & 2:

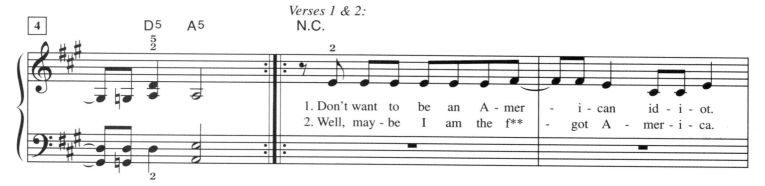

1. Don't want to be an A - mer - i - can id - i - ot.
2. Well, may - be I am the f** - got A - mer - i - ca.

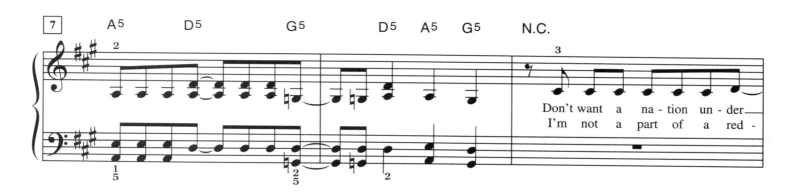

Don't want a na - tion un - der
I'm not a part of a red -

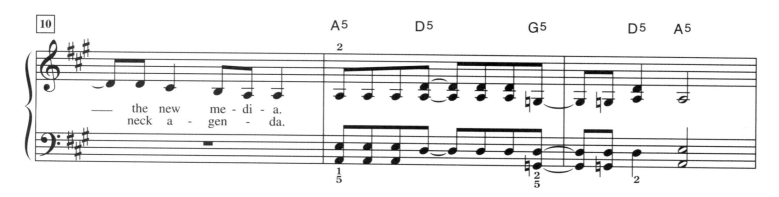

— the new me - di - a.
neck a - gen - da.

REDUNDANT

Arranged by Carol Matz

Lyrics by Billie Joe
Music by Billie Joe and Green Day

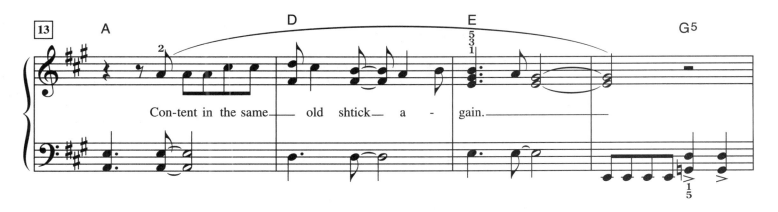

Con-tent in the same old shtick a - gain.

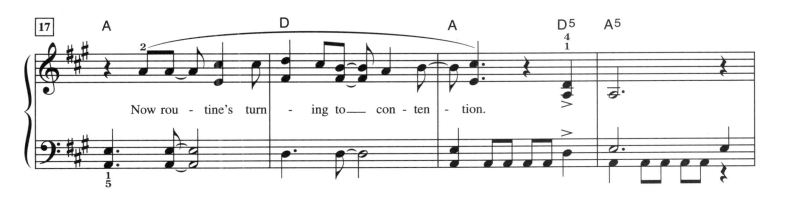

Now rou - tine's turn - ing to con - ten - tion.

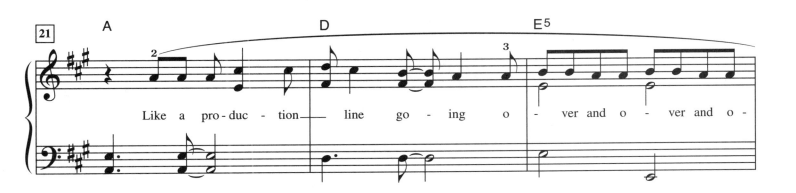

Like a pro-duc - tion line go - ing o - ver and o - ver and o-

Chorus:

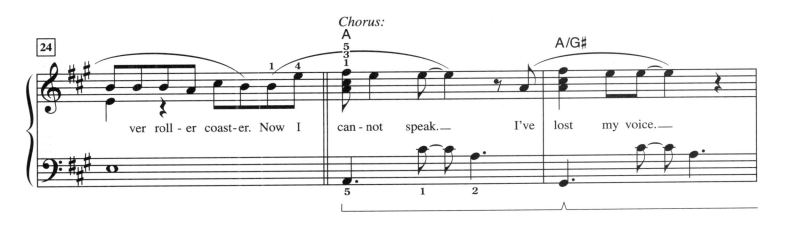

ver roll - er coast-er. Now I can - not speak. I've lost my voice.

60

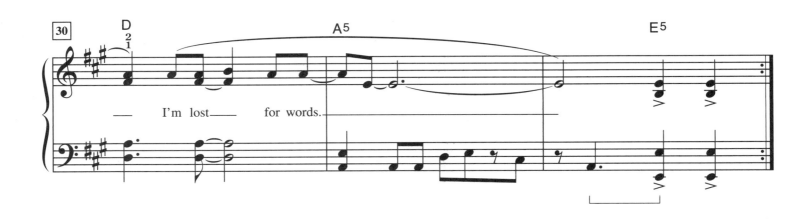

Verse 2:
Choreographed and lack of passion,
Prototypes of what we were.
One full circle till I'm nauseous.
Taken for granted now.
I waste it, faked it, ate it. Now I hate it.
Cause I... *(to Chorus)*